The Lion Pride

Gina Cline   Traci Dibble

This is a lion family.

There are baby lions.

The baby lions sleep.

The baby lions play.

A lion family can have
many baby lions.

This is a lion dad.

There can be two or three
lion dads in a lion family.

hyena

The lion dads look out for these animals.

They will eat what a lion eats.

They will eat a lion.

The lion dad has to stop them.

This is a lion mom.

There can be lots of lion moms in a lion family.

The lions have to eat.

Some of the lion moms go out.

They look for animals to eat.

They look and look.
They see a zebra.

The lion moms will get a zebra to eat.

They make a circle.

They jump on the zebra.

They have the zebra.
But they will not eat it.

The lion dads will eat.

Then the lion moms will eat.

Then the baby lions get to eat.

Now the lions will sleep.

They will not eat for two or three days.

Where Lions Live

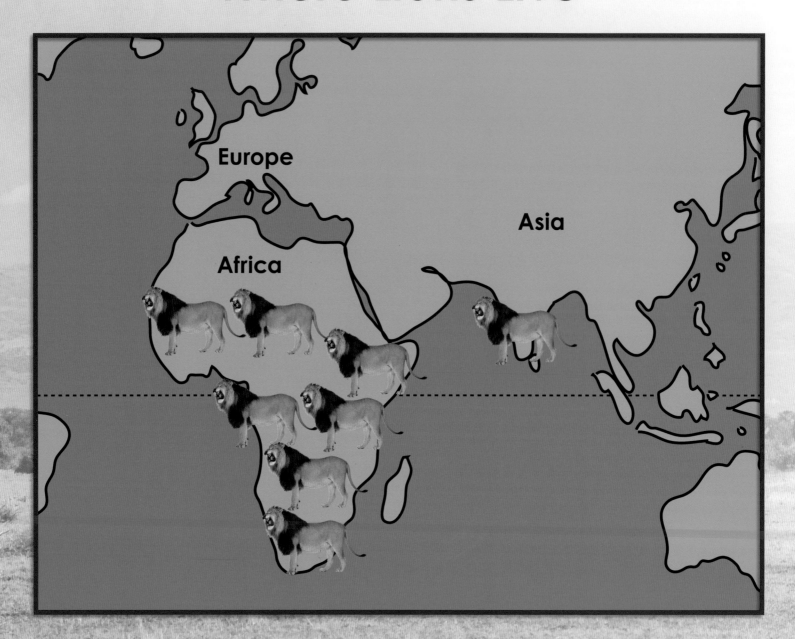

The Lion's Body Parts

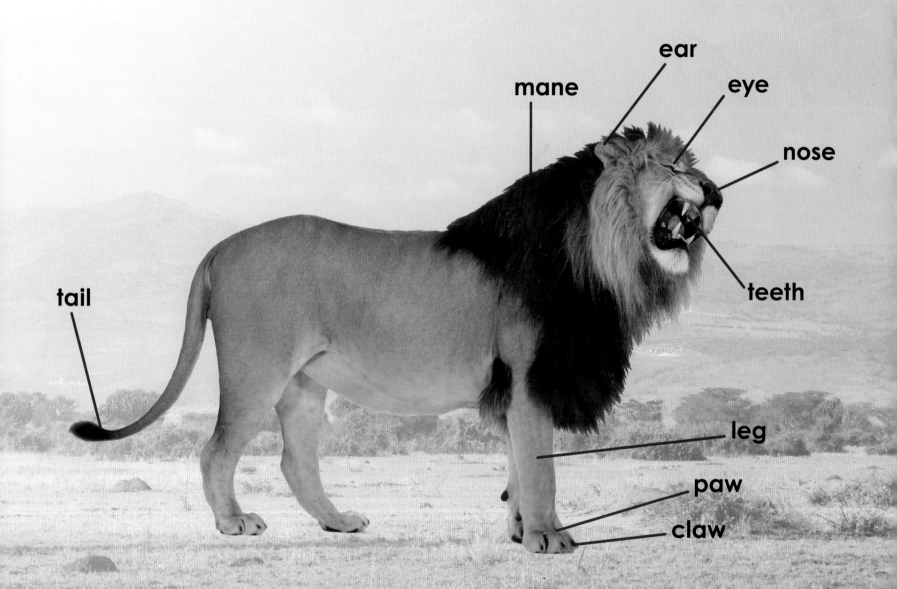

ear

mane

eye

nose

teeth

tail

leg

paw

claw

The Lion's Food Web

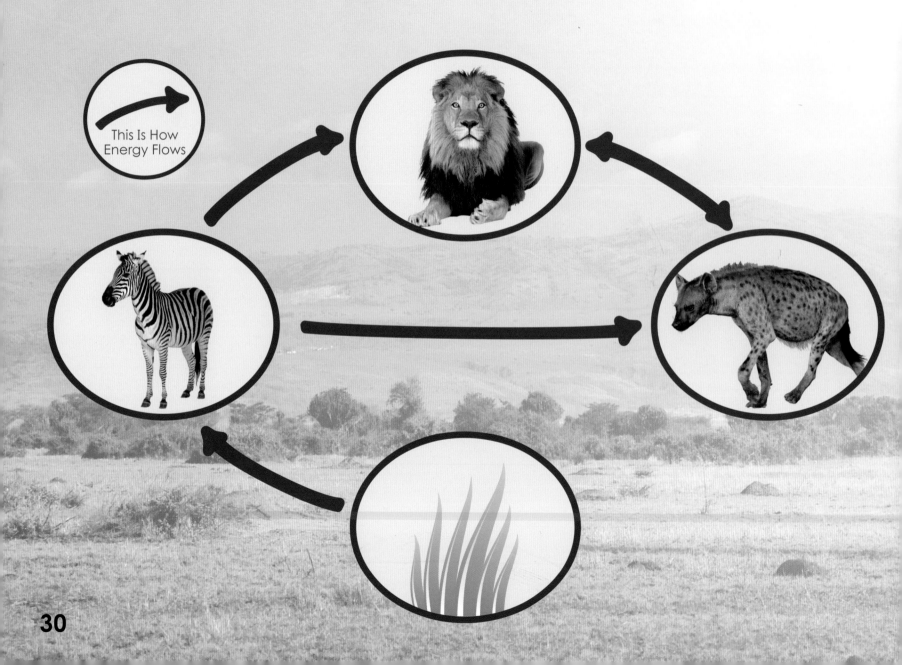

This Is How Energy Flows

The Lion's Life Cycle

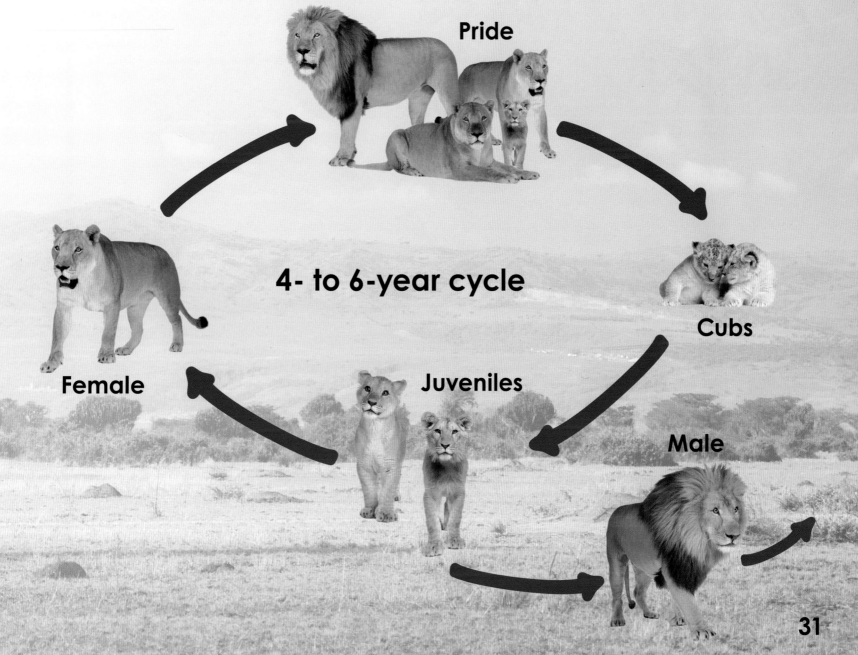

Pride

Cubs

4- to 6-year cycle

Female

Juveniles

Male

Power Words

How many can you read?

a	can	get	jump	now	some	they
and	circle	go	look	of	stop	this
animal	dad	has	lots	on	the	three
are	day	have	make	or	them	to
baby	eat	in	many	out	then	two
be	family	is	mom	play	there	what
but	for	it	not	see	these	will